I0755160

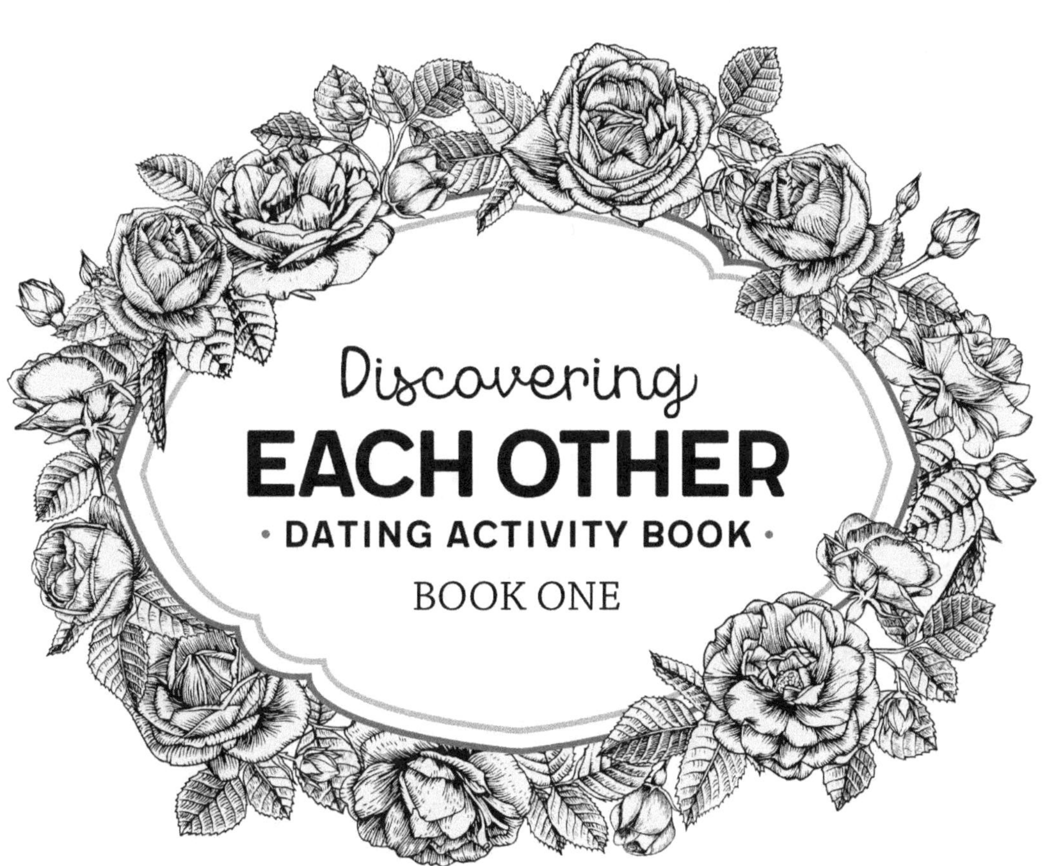
Discovering
EACH OTHER
• DATING ACTIVITY BOOK •
BOOK ONE

Welcome To The

# Discovering Each Other Dating Activity Book

Book One

Do you want to avoid this dating dilemma?

*"So what are we going to do on our date?"*

*"I don't know, what do you want to do?"*

You can help turn your time together into a lively, entertaining experience by getting copies of the *Discovering Each Other Dating Activity Book One* for you and your date.

**What's the book about?**
*The Discovering Each Other Dating Activity Book One* is the first in a series of books that is designed to help couples have an exciting time together while exploring and strengthening their relationship. Discovering Each Other Dating Activity Book One is designed for couples that are just starting to get to know each other.

**What's in the book?**
*The Discovering Each Other Dating Activity Book One* contains a series of drawing, coloring and other activities to help you share your background, romantic interests and together, to complete numerous exercises that research has shown can improve satisfaction in your relationship.

**Do you publish other books like this?**
This book is part of the Drawing Closer Together™ series for each step in building and sustaining a relationship. Whether you are just starting out in a new relationship, getting serious with someone or even looking to reignite the spark in a long-term relationship, Inward Vistas will be publishing a book that addresses these stages of a relationship.

**Anything else we should know?**
The books in the Drawing Closer Together™ series are not intended to serve as any form or substitute for couple or individual therapy or medical treatment. Seek professional help immediately for such concerns.

**Ok, we're ready.**
Great! First, check out the the How It Works FAQ to see an example of an activity, then get started diving into the activities with your date.

# How it Works FAQ

This book includes variety of activities, all designed to help you get to know your date in a fun manner. Here's one activity you'll do together.

**Step 1:** Read the question and think of your answer.

**Are you a cat or dog kind of person?**

**Step 2:** COLOR, DRAW or write Your answer

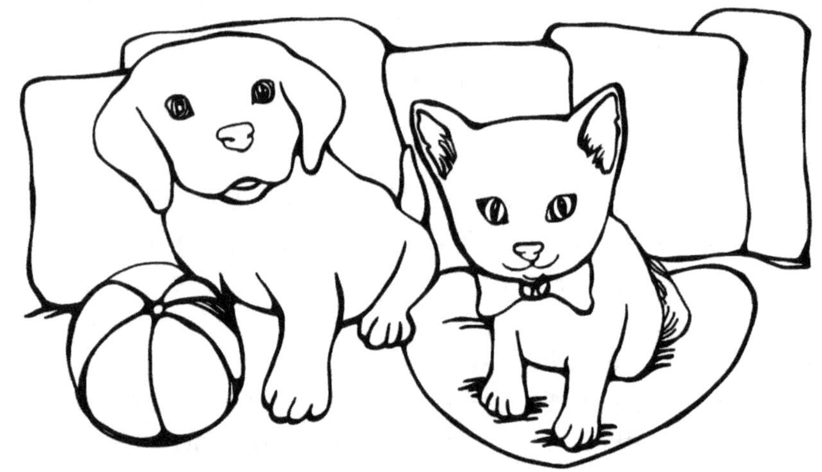

**Step 3:** Share your answer to the follow-up question at the bottom of the page and your drawing with your date.

**How important is it for you to have a pet?**

# Are you concerned about?

## I'm not an artist, I can't draw ...

That's okay. If you can draw a sort of straight line, a mostly round circle or a triangle, you can draw well enough to experience the fun and closeness that the Drawing Closer Together™ books are designed to foster.

## Maybe my date won't want to do this

Maybe, but maybe your date is also wondering what to do on your upcoming *"I want everything to go right but I'm so nervous"* date.

The Drawing Closer Together Dating Activity books take the pressure off both of you by providing engaging activities to help you easily get to know each other.

## Do we need to buy two books, one for each of us?

The best experience will be for each of you to use your own copy of the book as most activities in the book are designed for each person to use their own copy of the book. Or, one person could use a blank piece of paper instead of using a second copy of the book.

Regardless, please respect the copyright and avoid making copies of the book or pages within.

## Should we complete the activities in page number order?

The activities are listed in an organized fashion but feel free to start with those the two of you feel most comfortable with and then complete the remaining activities.

## Do we need an expensive colored pencil set?

Nope. You can snag a few colored pencils, crayons or pens from home.

*Discovering Each Other*
*Dating Activity Book*
Book One

This is a Drawing Closer Together™ book
Published by Inward Vistas



This edition printed in 2016 by Inward Vistas LLC, 2906 Central Avenue, Suite 252, Evanston, Illinois 60201



ISBN: 1-945037-06-7
ISBN 13: 978-1-945037-06-1

10 9 8 7 6 5 4 3 2 1

Printed and bound in the United States of America.

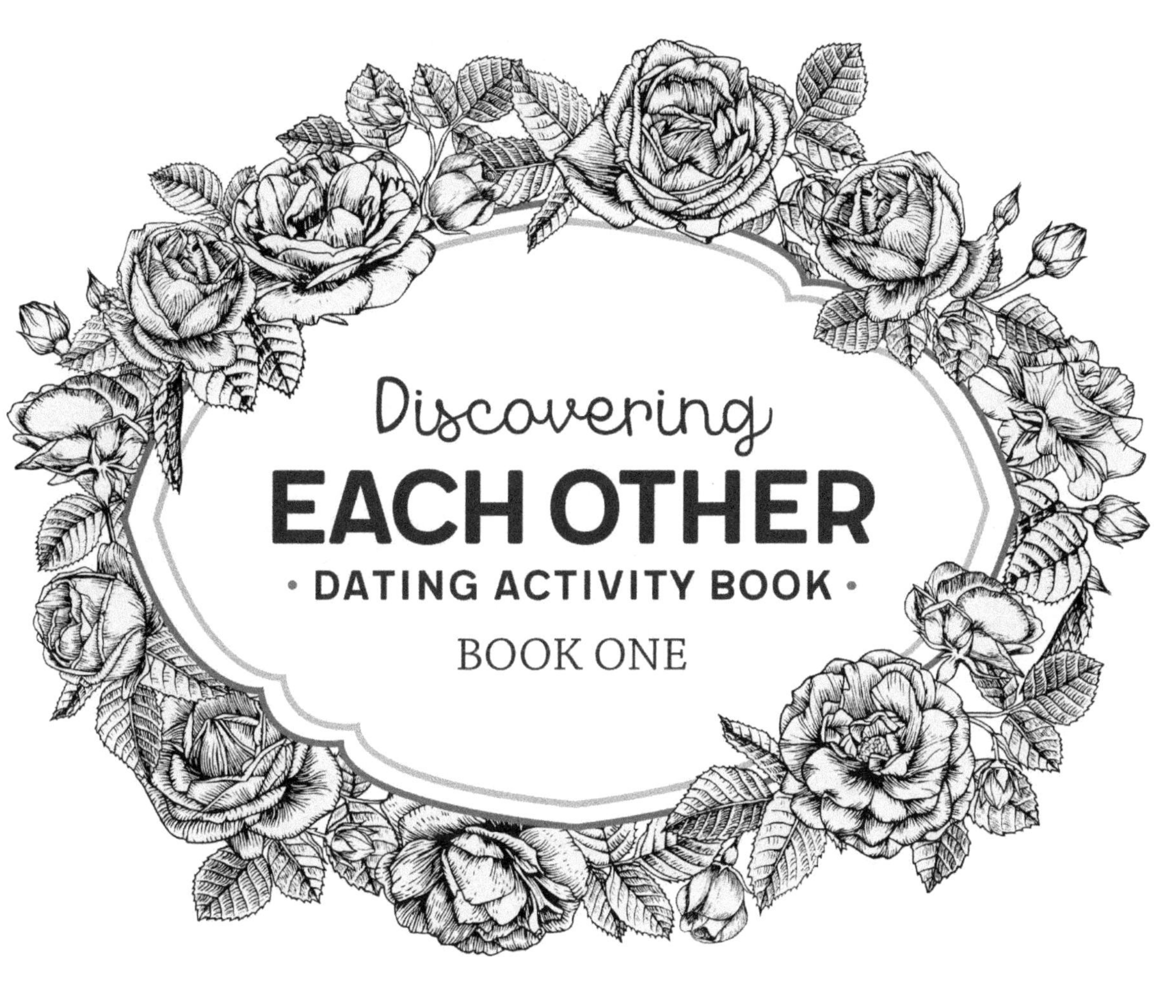


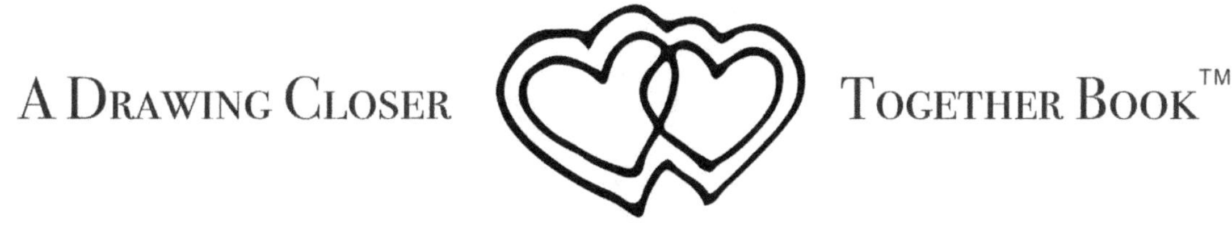


ELLE DAHLMAN, M. A.

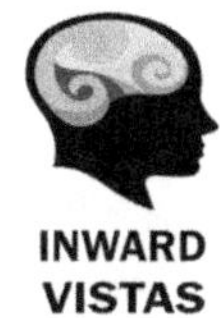

# SHARING A GREAT EXPERIENCE YOU'VE HAD HELPS OTHERS KNOW WHAT YOU ENJOY.

Start with thinking about the most awesome place you've visited.
Draw something that symbolizes that place for you.

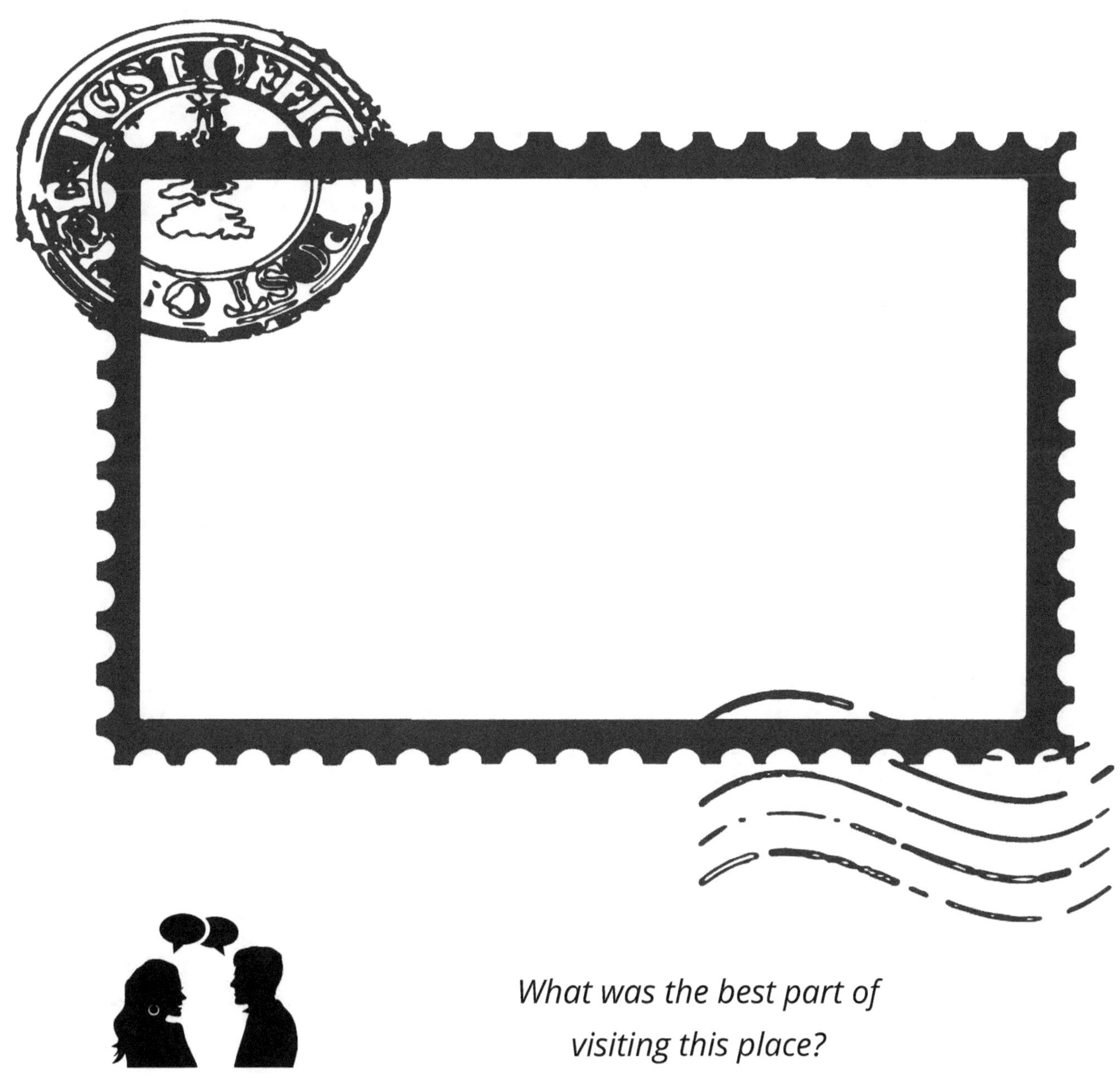

*What was the best part of visiting this place?*

# Have you dreamed of traveling the world?

Color in the areas of the top five places you hope to visit in your lifetime.

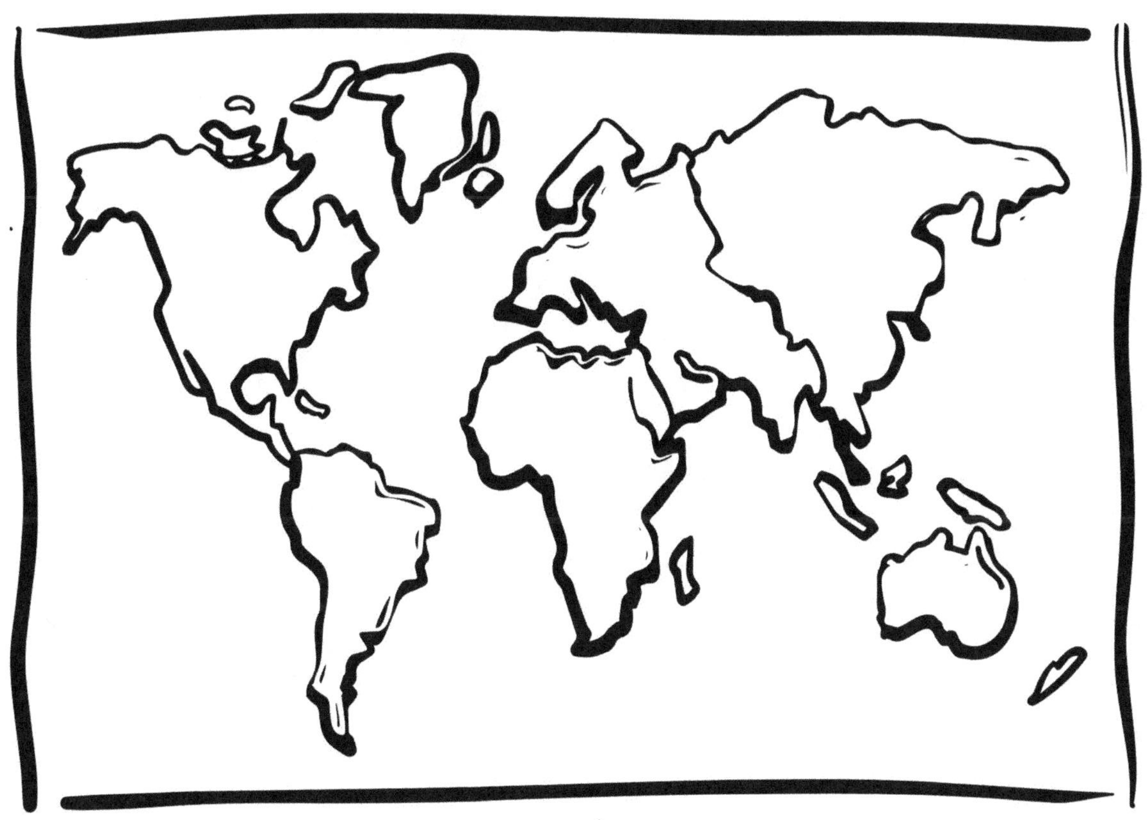

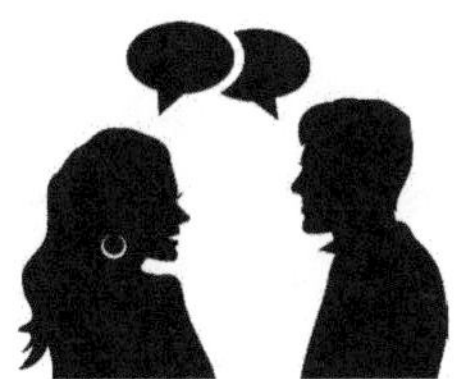

*Share what you would enjoy most about visiting these places.*

  

# HAVING A HEATED DRINK ON A DATE CAN BE TRULY HEARTWARMING.

Color the picture below to depict your favorite warm drink.

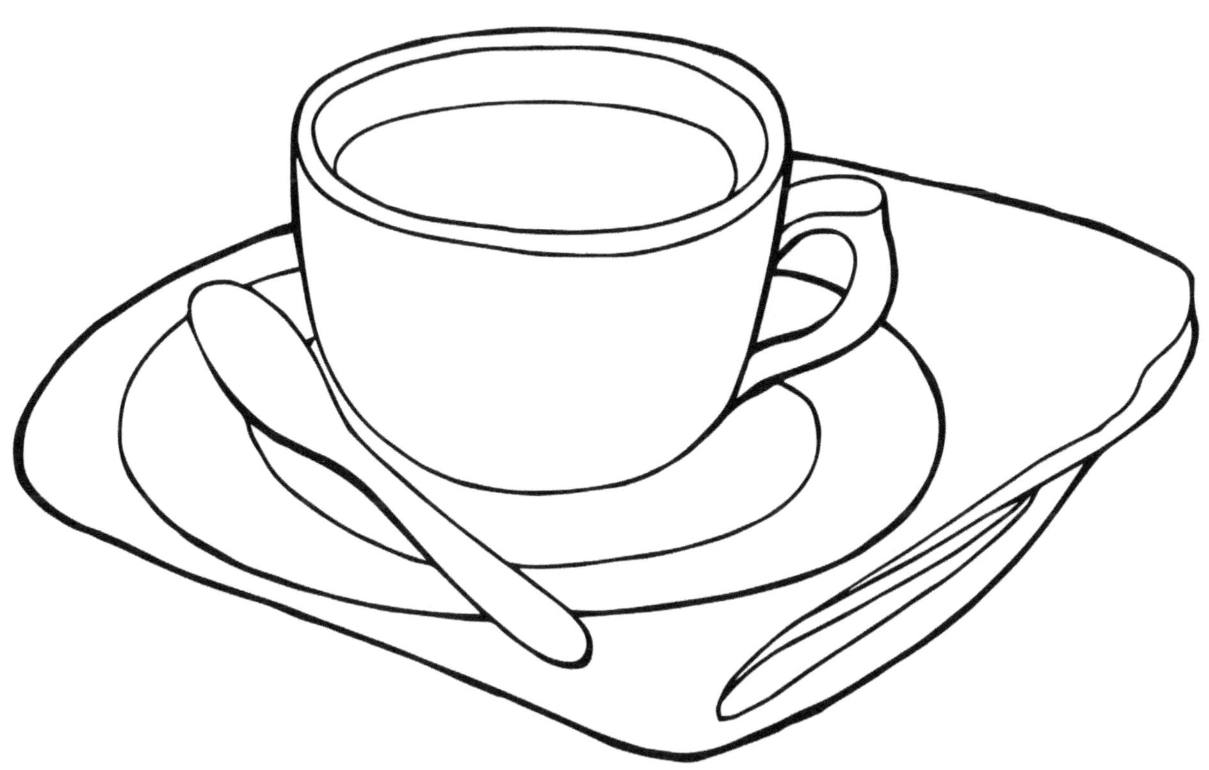

If you can make or order your favorite warm drink right now, go ahead and do it.

(This is known to be a good thing to do on a date.)

  

# WORK TOGETHER TO WRITE A SENTENCE THAT CAPTURES A BELIEF BOTH OF YOU SHARE ABOUT DATING.

You'll need to chat first about your feelings about dating before beginning to compose your sentence. Have your sentence start with the words *Dating is for* and also include the word *because* somewhere in the sentence.

Dating is for

______________________________

______________________________

because

______________________________

______________________________

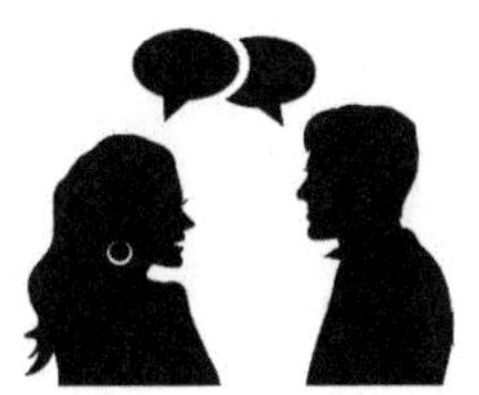

*Do you think that each of you is seeking compatible experiences from a relationship?*

  

**Read all the instructions below before proceeding.**

**Tear out this page from one of your books and use it to make a paper airplane. The catch is that each of you has to take turns in folding the same piece of paper into an airplane.**

**Then take your creation on a test flight.**

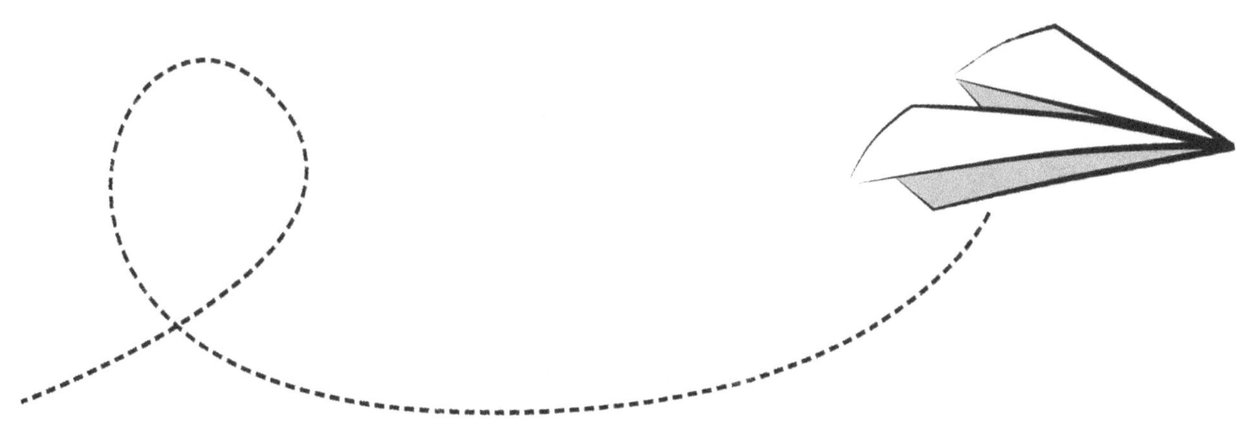

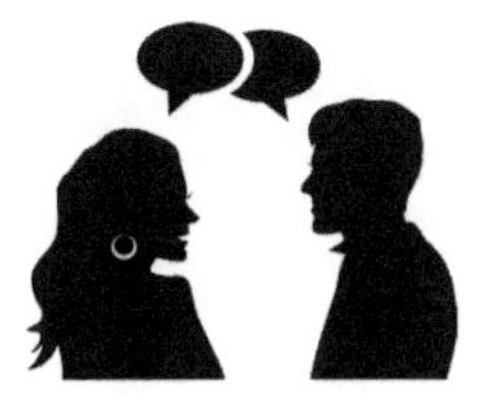

*How well did you work together to craft the plane?*

  

# NOW YOU'RE GOING TO PLAY A CROSSWORD PUZZLE TYPE GAME – WITHOUT USING ANY LINES OR HINTS.

Decide which one of you will go first and use that person's book for this game. That person will start by writing the name of one of their favorite foods in the middle of the page in a horizontal direction.

Next, the other person writes the name of one of their favorite foods in a vertical direction, using a letter from the first person's food item. Keep going, writing the names of your favorite foods until each of you has added six words. It should look like a crossword puzzle when you are done.

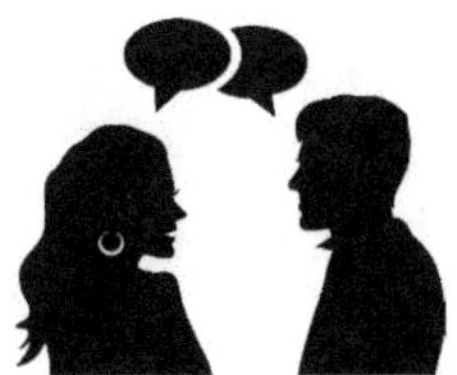

*How many food items were listed that both of you enjoy eating?*

  

# WHAT ARE YOUR FAVORITE TYPES OF MOVIES?

Color in the bags of popcorn above the movie genres that describe the types of movies you love to watch.

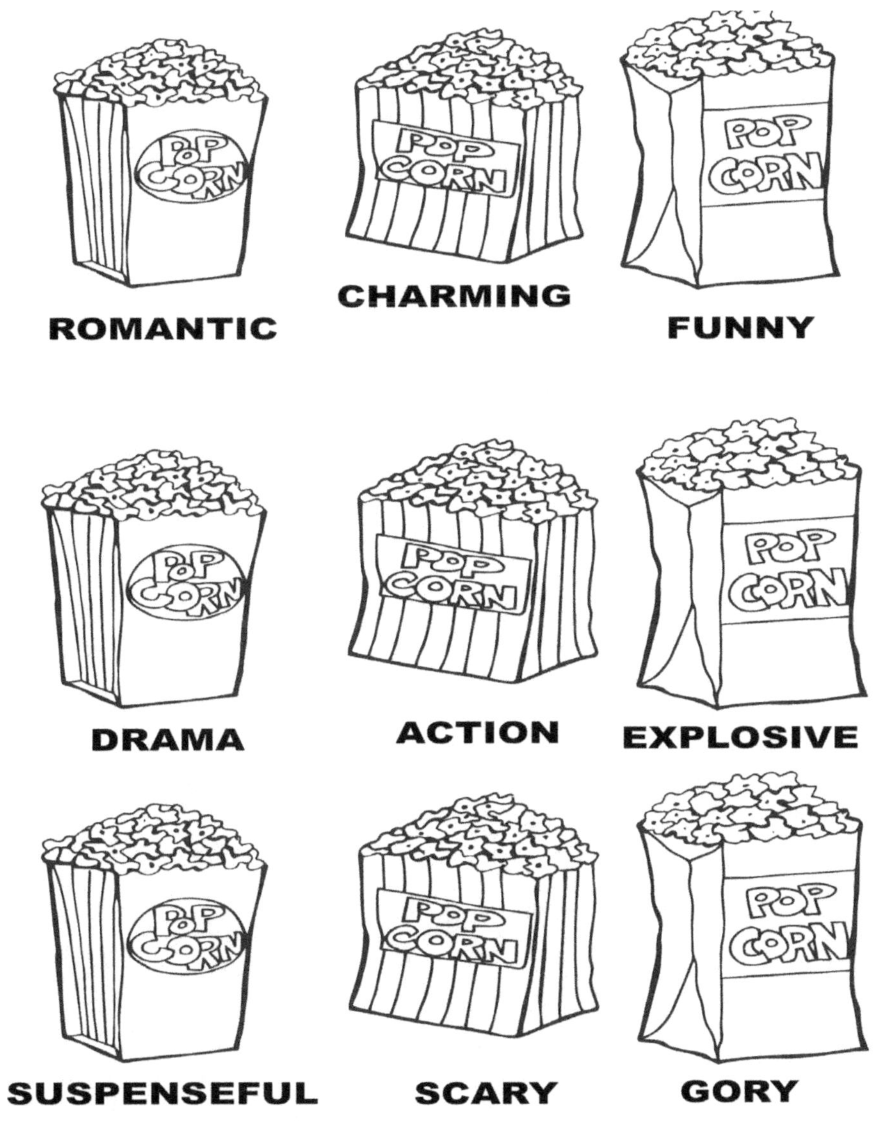


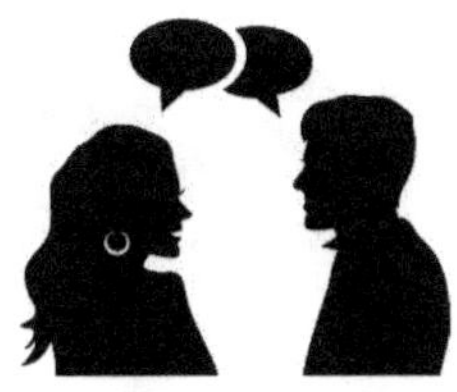

*Which of the genres your date chose would you also be interested in seeing?*

# WOULD YOU RATHER LIVE A SIMPLE LIFE IN A RURAL AREA OR EXPERIENCE THE EXCITEMENT OF CITY LIFE?

Color in the scene that describes the lifestyle you prefer.

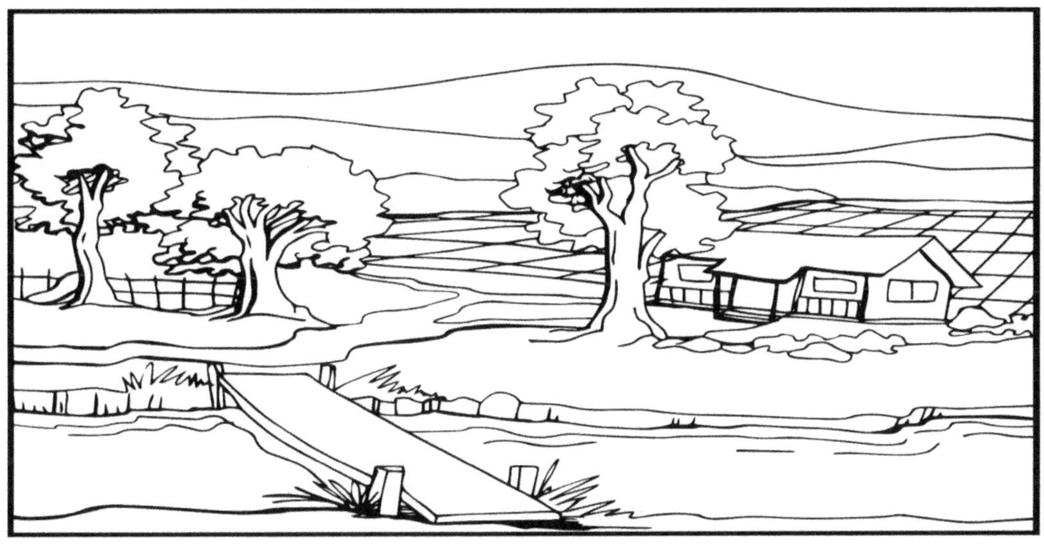

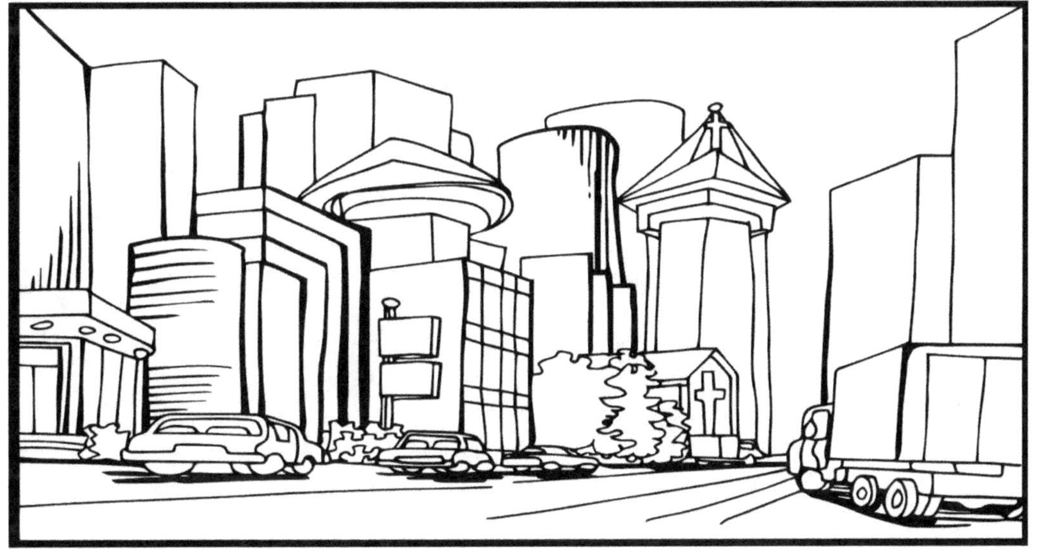

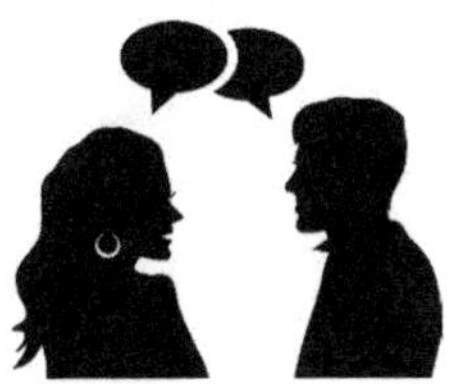

*What do you appreciate the most about your choice?*

# THINK OF SOMETHING YOU WERE TOO AFRAID TO TRY WHEN YOU WERE YOUNGER.

Now draw something that symbolizes that activity.

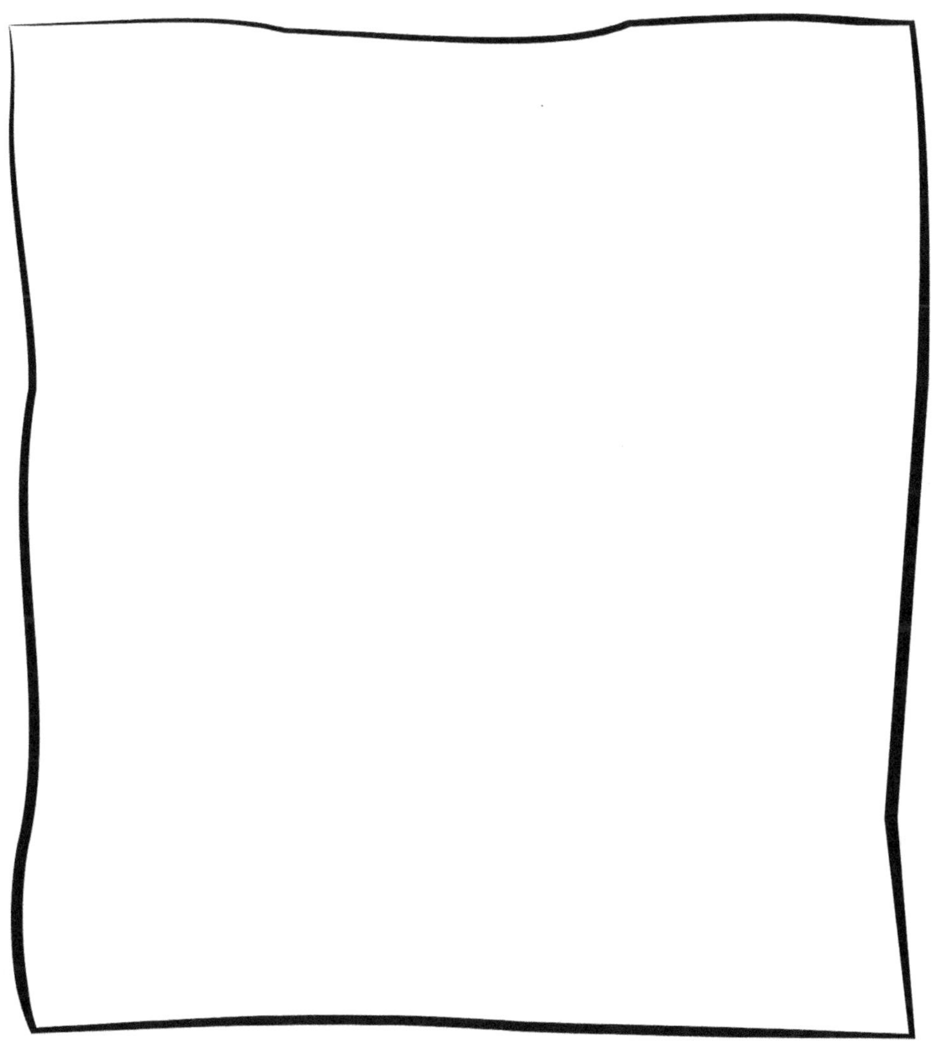

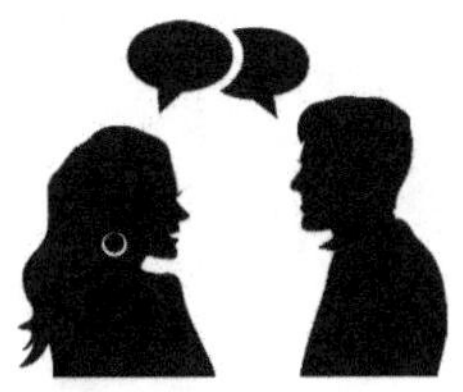

*Would you do it now if you had the chance?*
*Or, if you've already done it, congratulations!*
*Describe what it was like to overcome your fear.*

  

# ARE YOU A CAT OR DOG KIND OF PERSON?

Color in the type of animal you favor or add your favorite type of animal to the picture below.

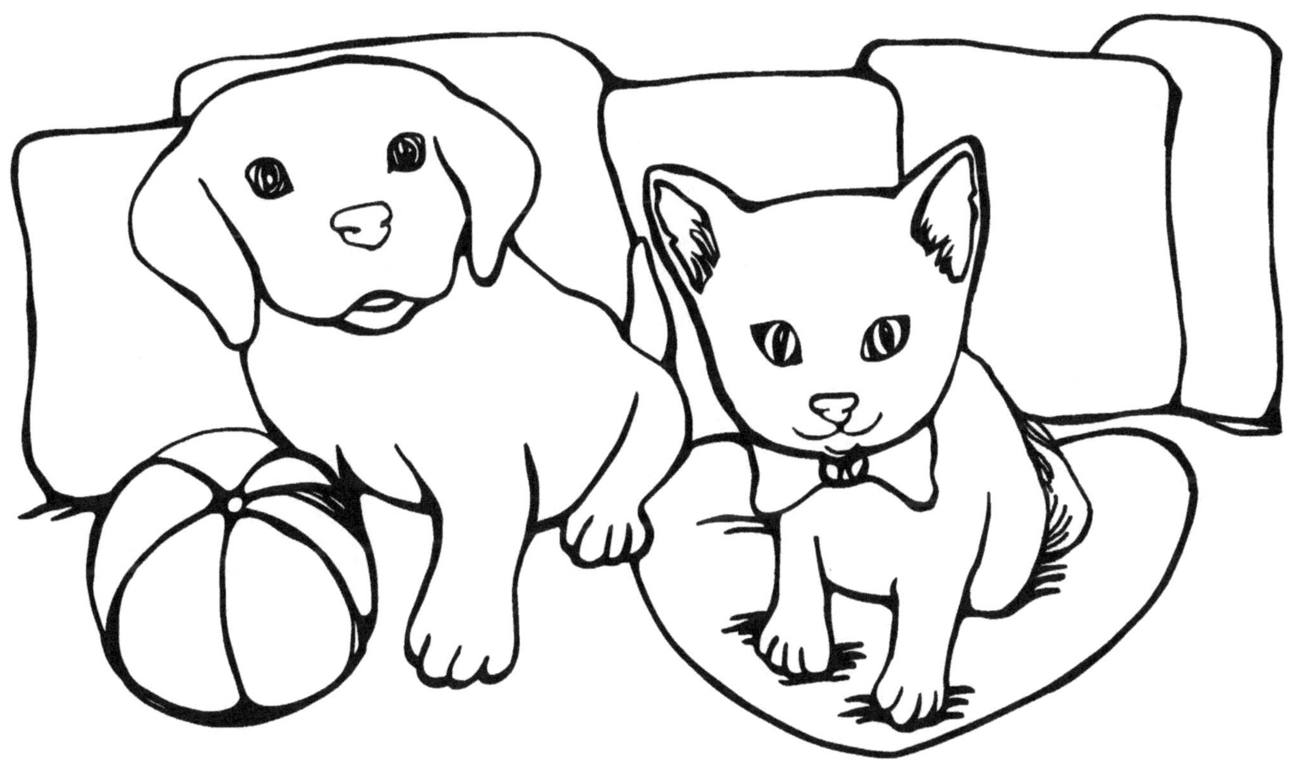

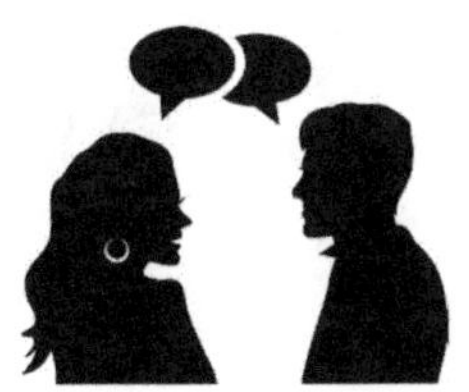

*How important is it for you to have a pet?*

# A GREAT WAY FOR PEOPLE TO UNDERSTAND EACH OTHER IS TO SHARE HOW THEY'VE OVERCOME ADVERSITY.

Draw an image of one of your accomplishments that required you to really push yourself beyond your normal limits.

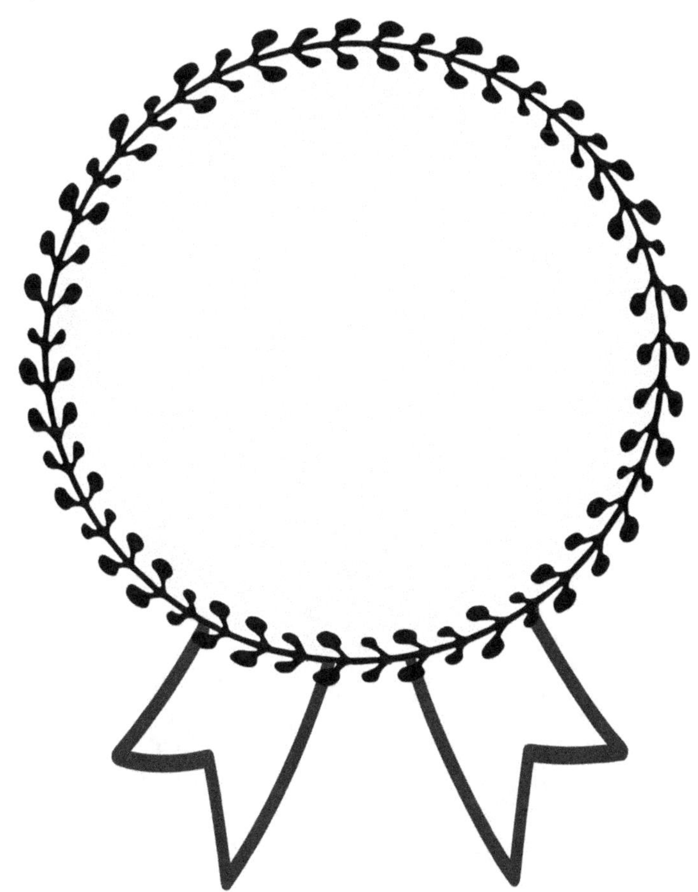

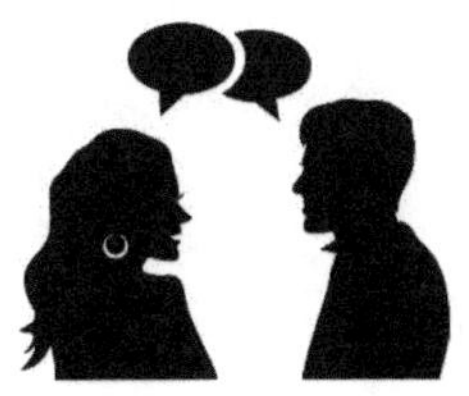

*Share a lesson you learned from the dedication you needed to achieve this accomplishment.*

  

**TO SHOW THE TYPES OF THINGS YOU VALUE IN YOUR LIFE, DRAW THE ONE ITEM** (not a person) **THAT YOU WOULD NOT WANT TO GIVE UP, EVEN IF YOU LOST EVERYTHING ELSE.**

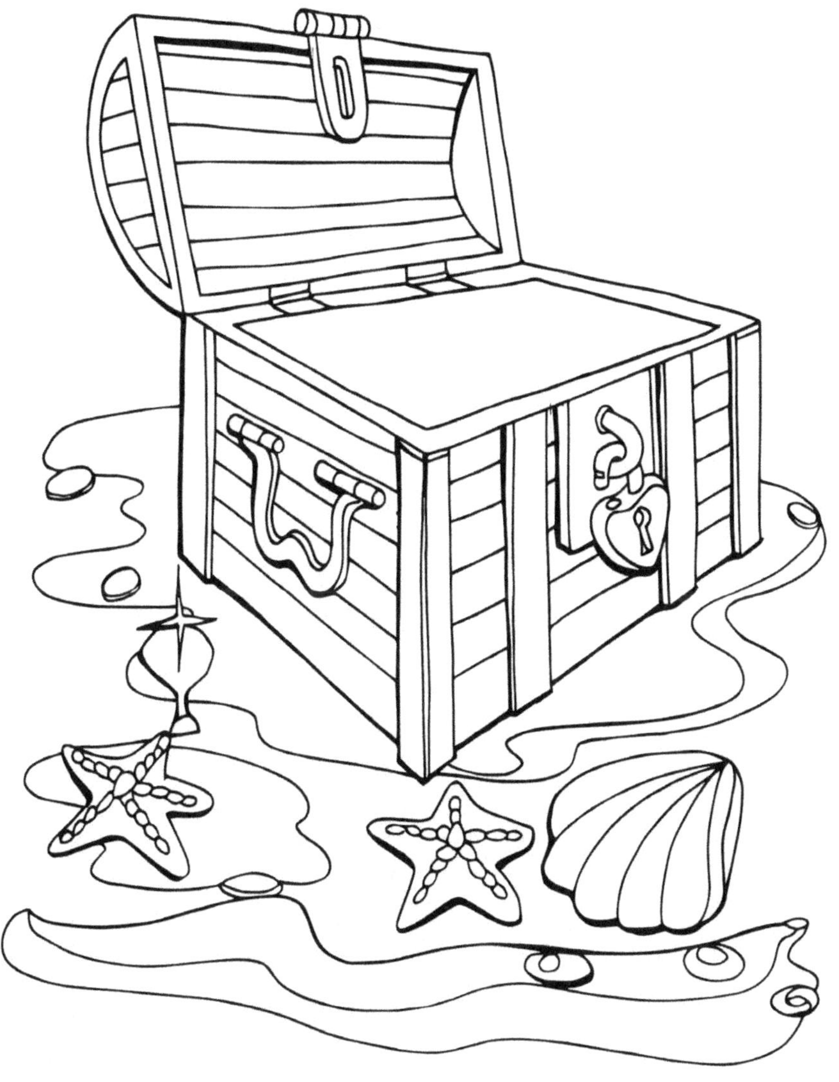

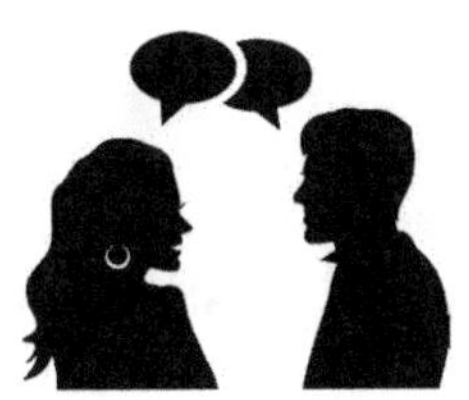

*Why do you cherish this item?*

  

# WE HAVE CHOICES ABOUT WHAT WE PURSUE IN LIFE.

Show which you would rather pursue at this point in your life – more money or more free time.
Draw more weights like the ones below on one side of the scale to show your preference.

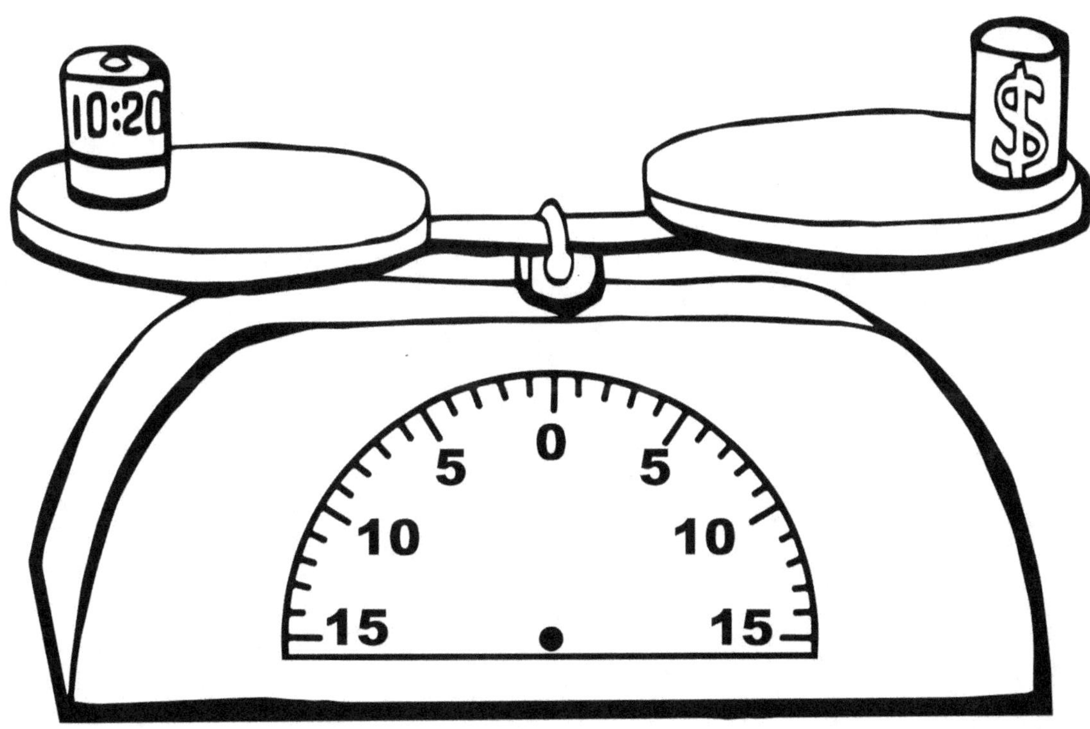


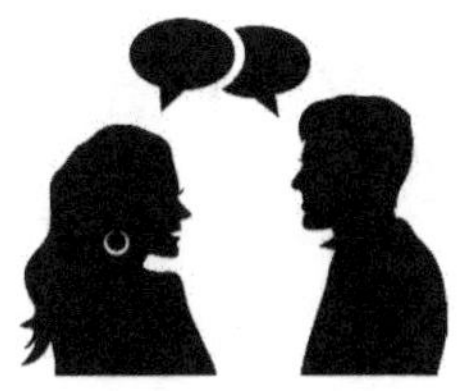

*What would you do with the extra money or free time?*

# GOOD FRIENDS KNOW EACH OTHER REALLY WELL, PERHAPS BETTER THAN WE KNOW OURSELVES.

Doodle one word or phrase that your friends would say really describes you.

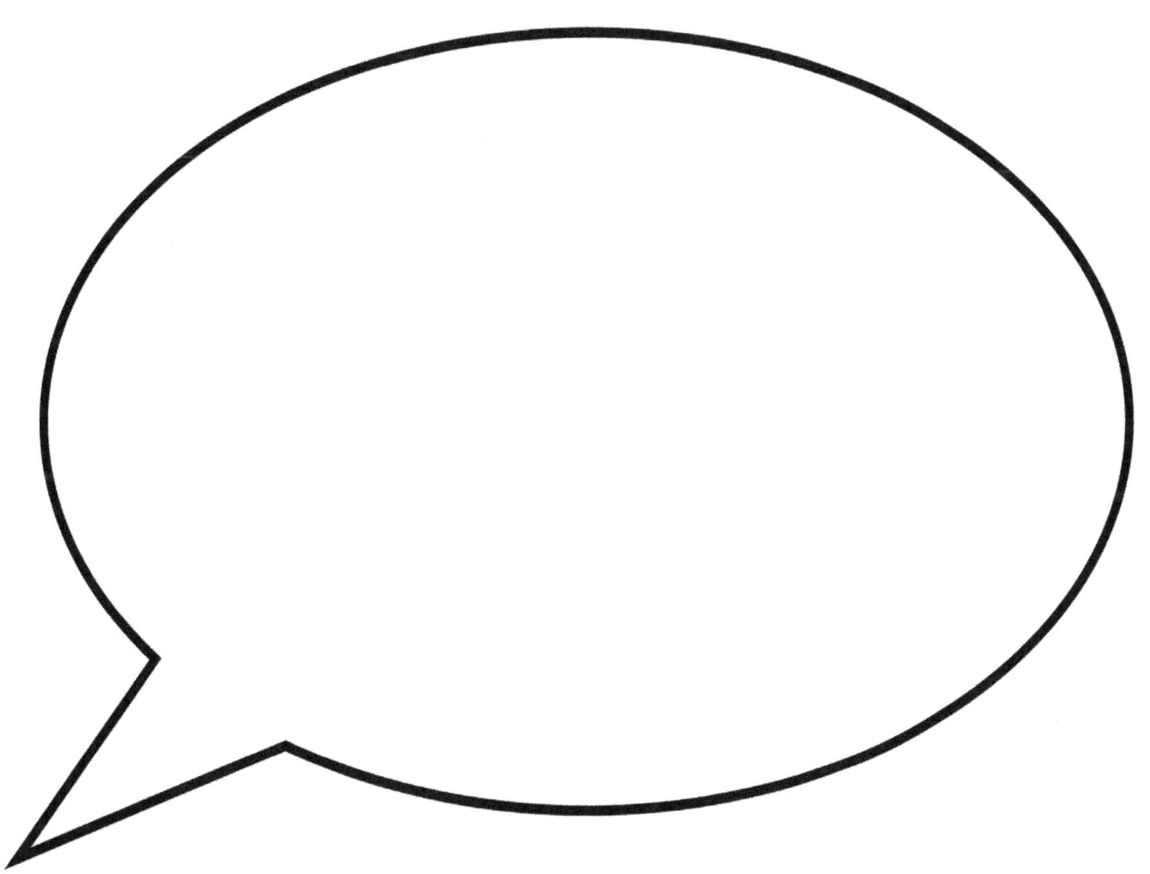

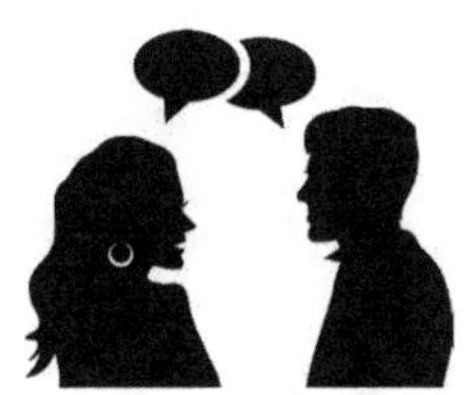

*Do you agree with them?*

  

# HAVE YOU EVER THOUGHT ABOUT HOW YOU WOULD CHANGE THE WORLD IF YOU WERE IN CHARGE?

Write on the scroll below an executive order you would issue if you were president of the United States for a day.

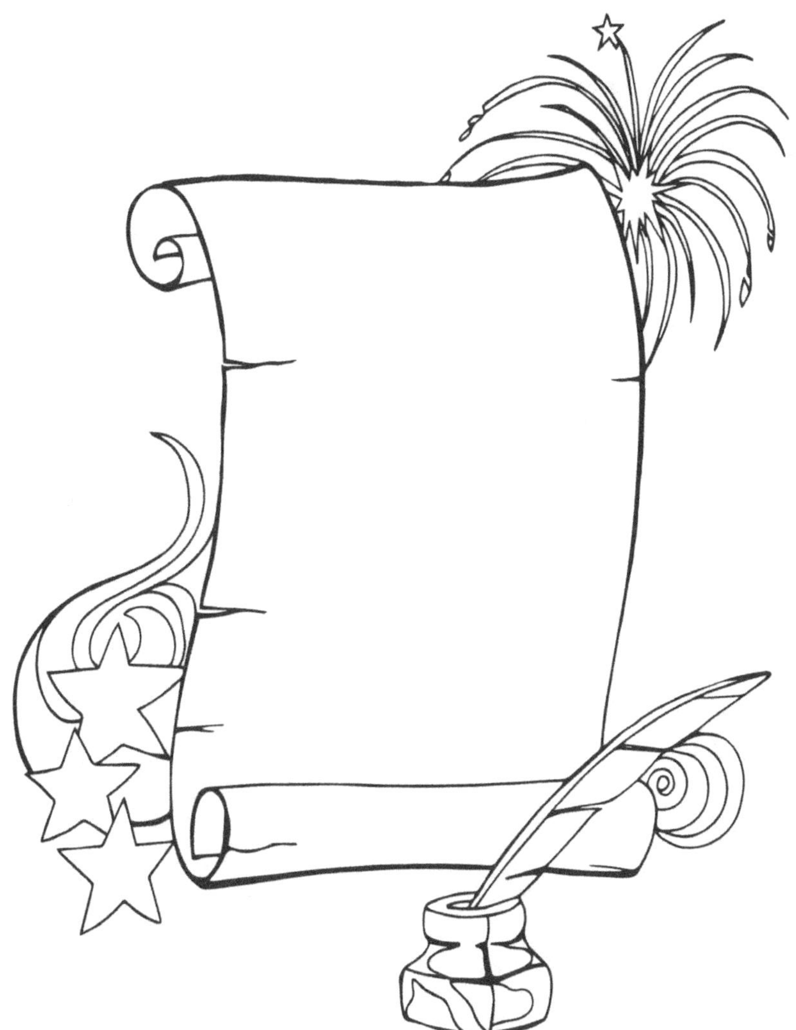

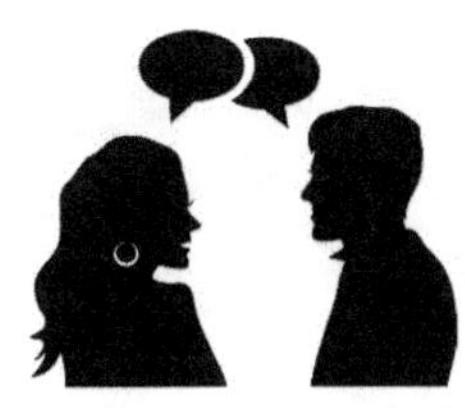

*Share why this topic is important to you.*

# Do you enjoy sports or physical exercise?

If so, inside the picture frame below write the names of or draw objects related to the sports or physical activities you enjoy.

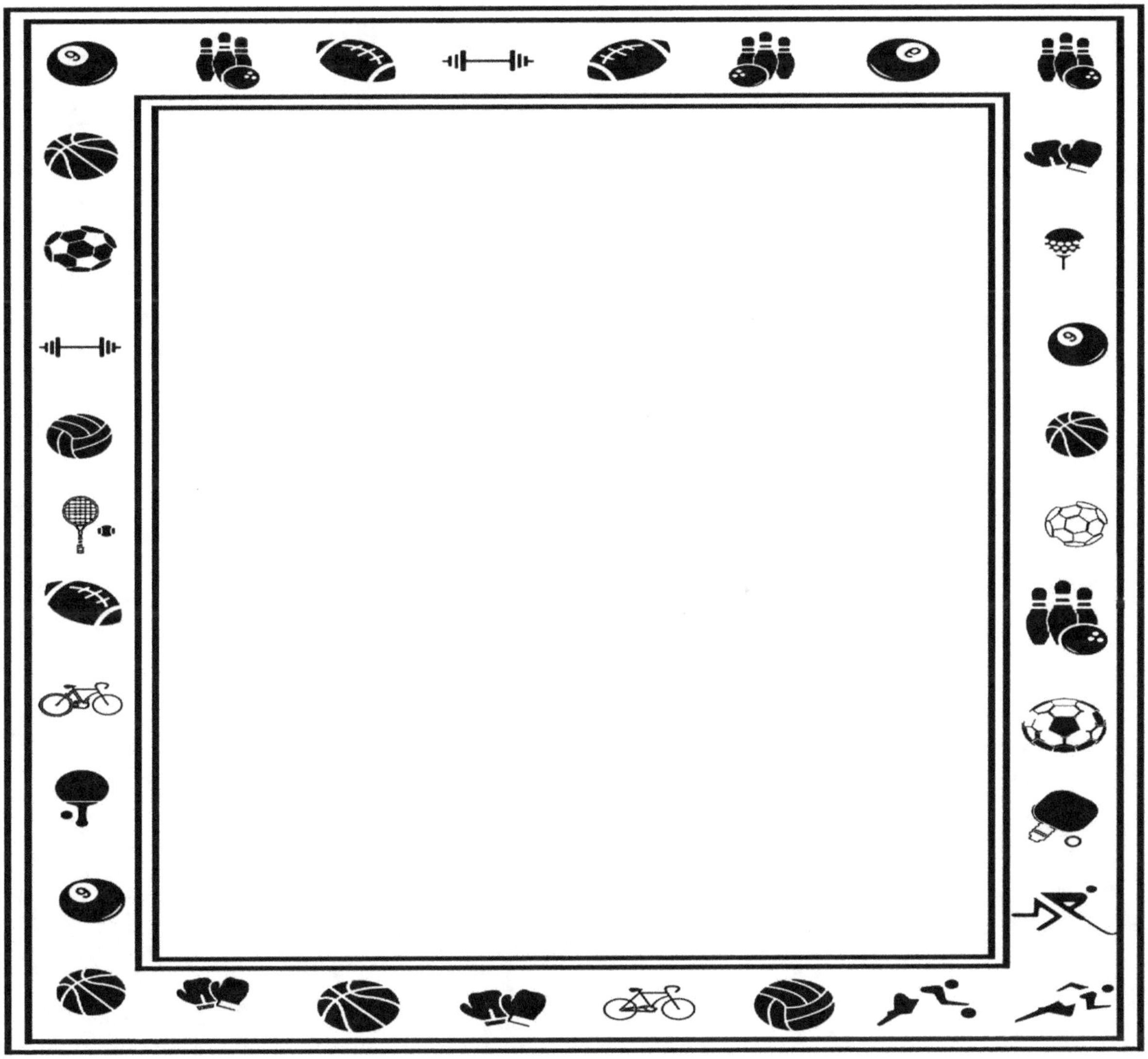

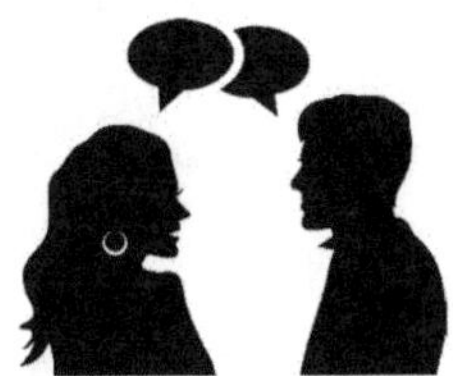

*Do you prefer performing or watching these activities?*

# TAKE A MOMENT TO THINK ABOUT YOUR BEST FRIENDS AND HOW THEIR FRIENDSHIP IS LIKE A GIFT.

Then pick a word that describes one thing you really appreciate about them and write that word inside the gift box.

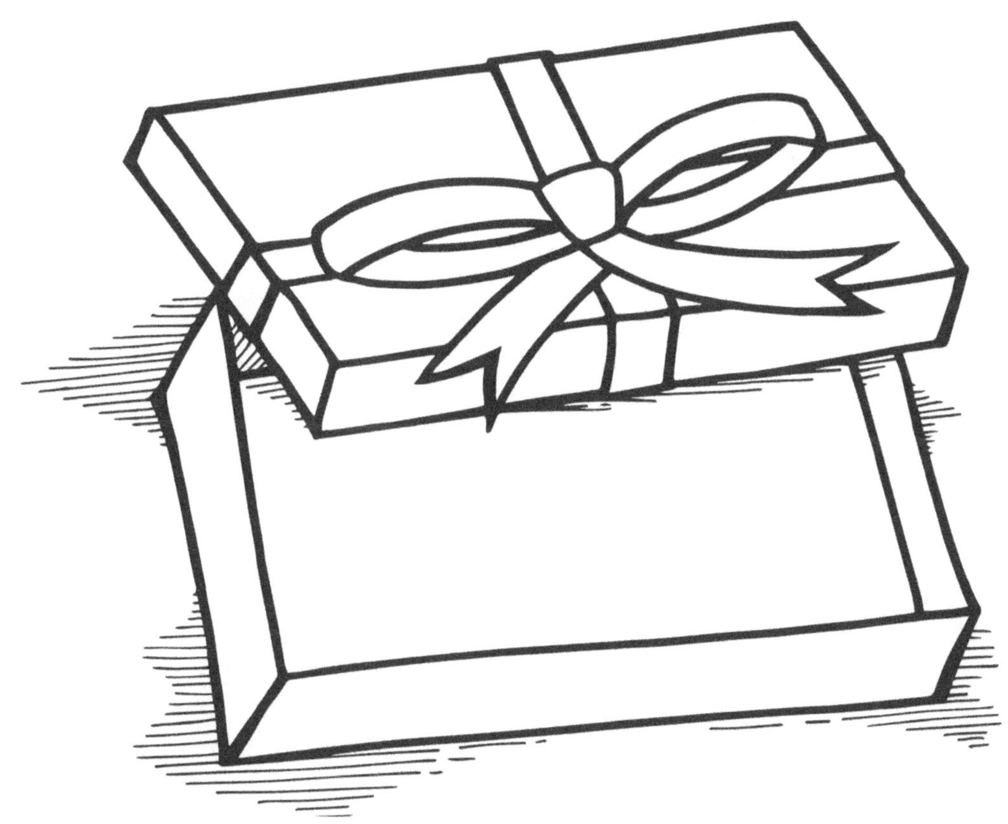

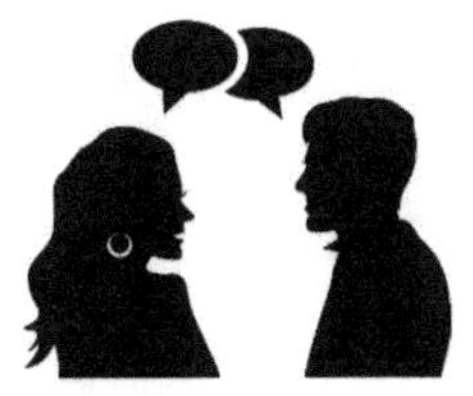

*Is this something you would also treasure in a romantic relationship?*

  

## Time to work together again. Get a timer, whether it's a watch, phone timer app, or clock, and get ready to time yourselves while playing a word game.

Set the timer to three minutes. Working together on one page, take three minutes to find words that are at least four letters long from the word *companionship*, and write them on the list below.

| 1. | 2. |
|---|---|
| 3. | 4. |
| 5. | 6. |
| 7. | 8. |
| 9. | 10. |
| 11. | 12. |
| 13. | 14. |
| 15. | 16. |
| 17. | 18. |
| 19. | 20. |

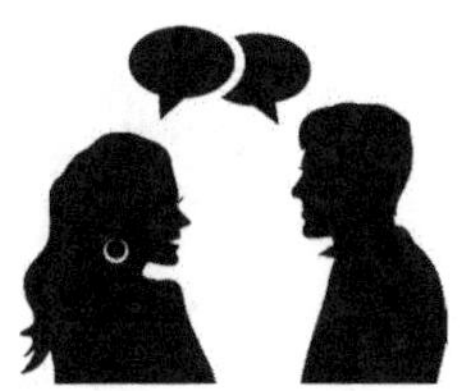

*How would you like to spend companionship time in a relationship?*

  

## SHARING THE GOALS THAT YOU HAVE SET FOR YOURSELF IS A GREAT WAY FOR PEOPLE TO UNDERSTAND WHERE YOU WANT TO GO IN LIFE.

Write a description of a goal you want to accomplish in the next year.

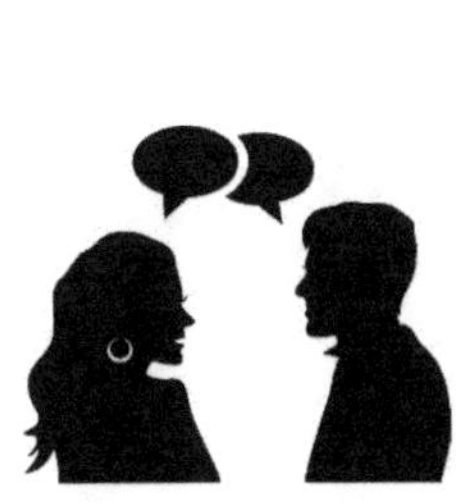

*How will accomplishing this goal change your perspective about yourself?*

# READY FOR A CHALLENGE WHILE SHARING SOMETHING ABOUT YOURSELF?

Place your pencil or crayon in the frame below, then without lifting it until you are done, draw an image that represents a simple talent or skill you have such as a magic trick, a song you can sing or quick dish you can cook.

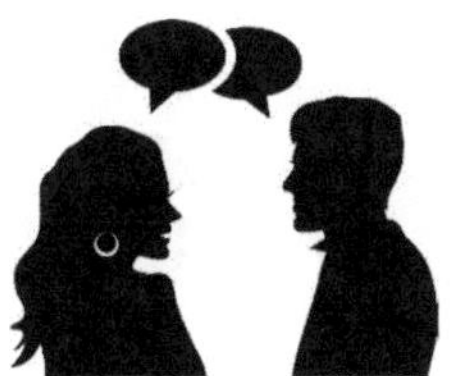

*Could you teach this skill to your date?*

# DRAW A PICTURE OF SOMETHING YOU REALLY ENJOY ABOUT YOUR WORK OR SCHOOL.

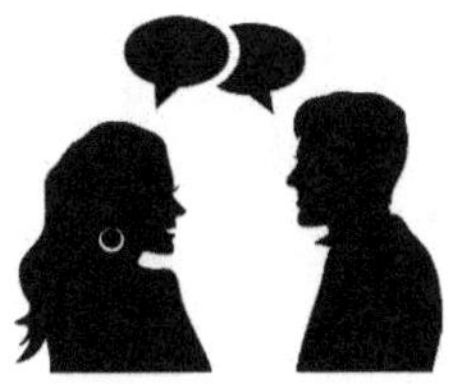

*What makes it gratifying?*

# WE CAN DEVELOP A STRONGER UNDERSTANDING OF EACH OTHER BY DESCRIBING OUR FAMILY BACKGROUNDS.

Using stick figures, show the family members you grew up with, including your parents, siblings, other relatives, and yourself, from youngest to oldest. Label each stick figure with the first name of the person it represents.

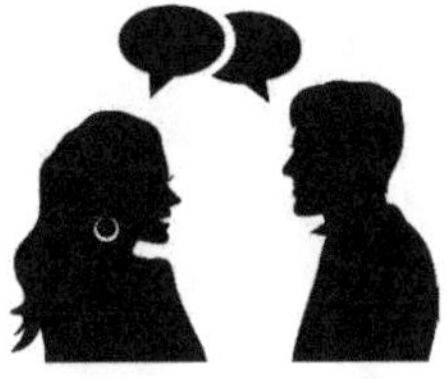

*What did you enjoy most about growing up in your birth order position (like first born, middle child, youngest or only child)?*

  

# DO YOU ENJOY THRILLING ADVENTURES OR RELAXING ACTIVITIES?

Color the image that represents the activity you would rather do on a Saturday afternoon.

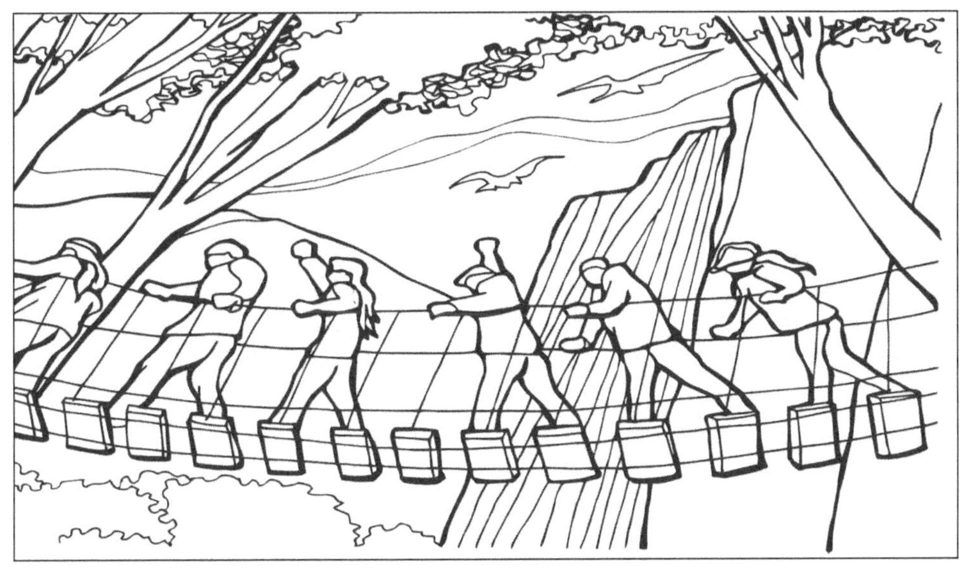

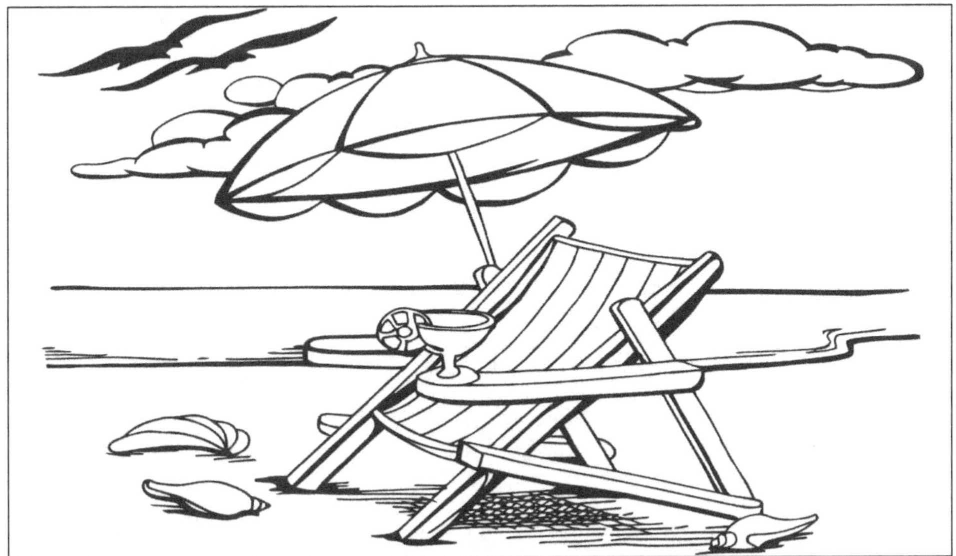

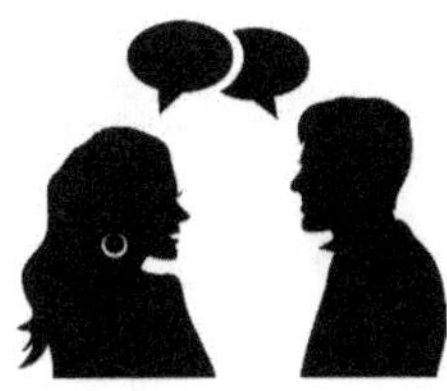

*What's your favorite daring or relaxing activity?*

  

# PEOPLE STARTING NEW RELATIONSHIPS CAN STILL BE JOURNEYING FROM OLD RELATIONSHIPS.

Color in the signs that describe your current relationship status or write your own description on the blank sign.

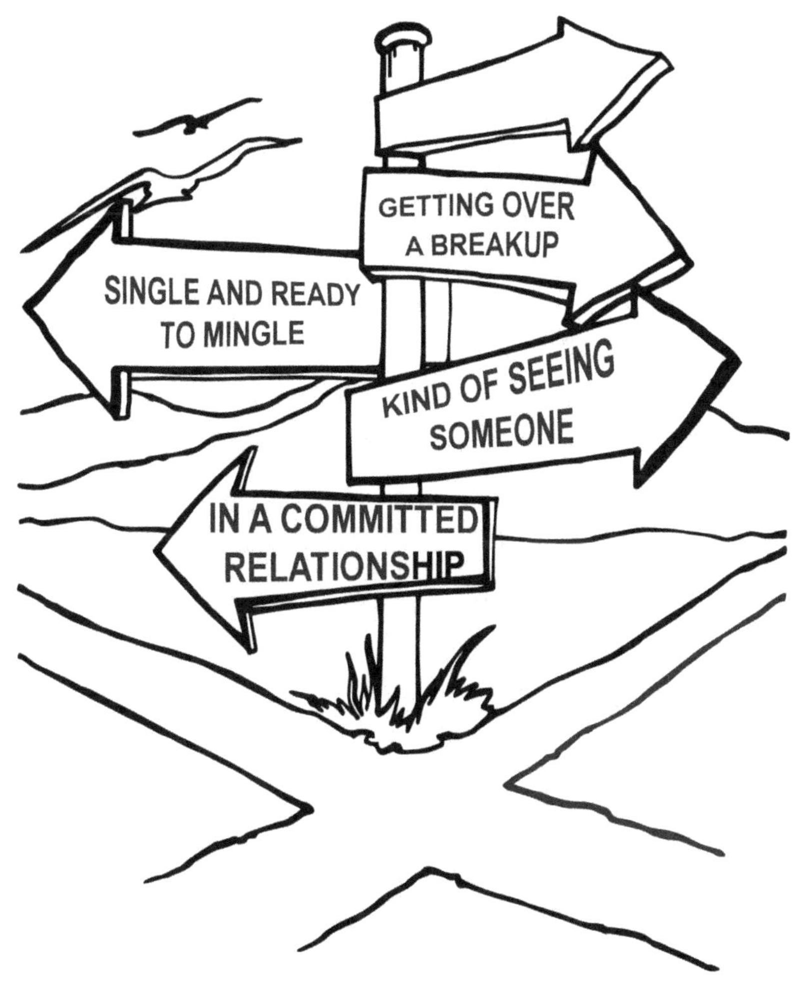


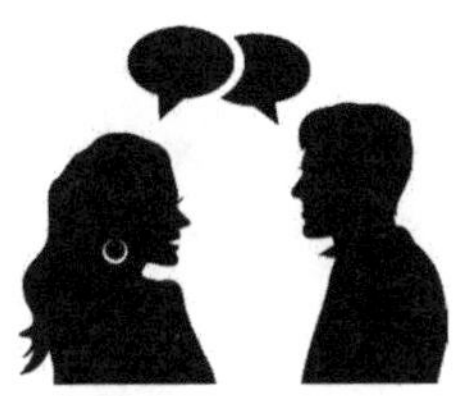

*Are you comfortable with your date's relationship status?*

# FIND A TIMER SUCH AS A WATCH, PHONE APP, OR CLOCK, AND SET THE TIMER FOR FOUR MINUTES.

Then get comfortably close to your date and start the timer. Now stare into their eyes.

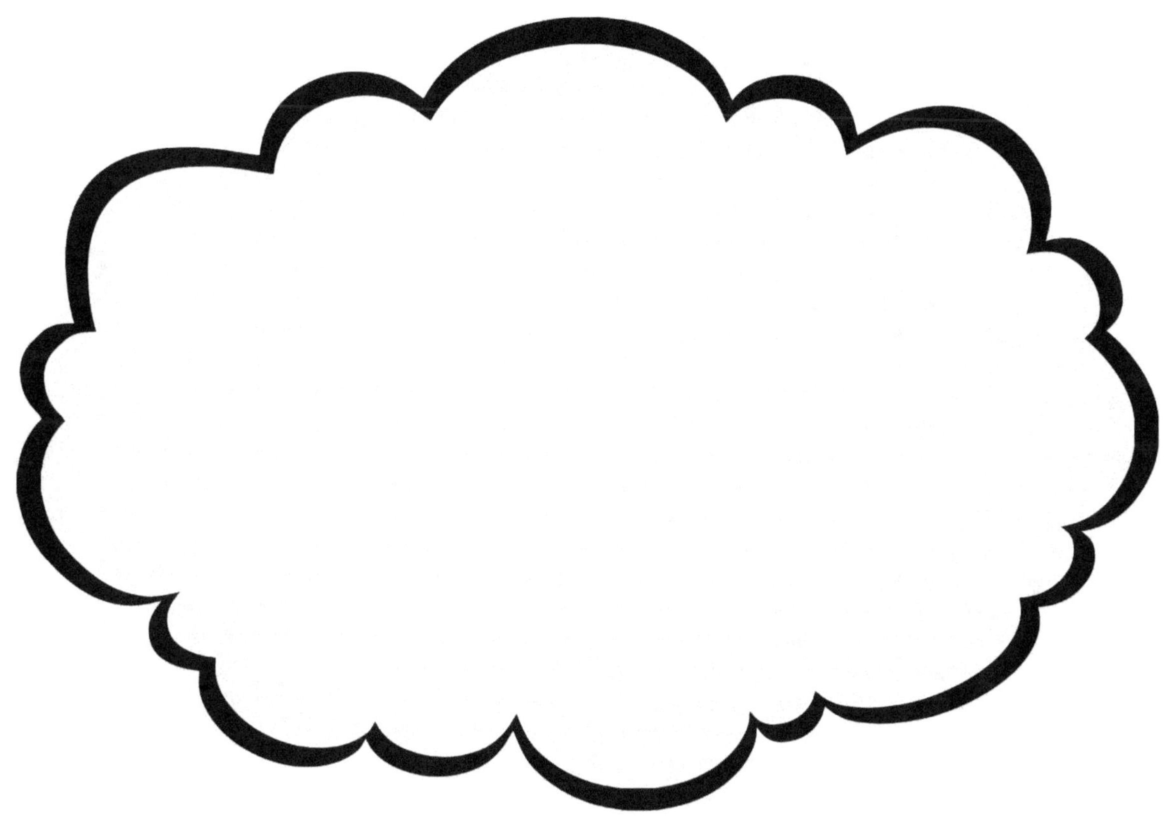

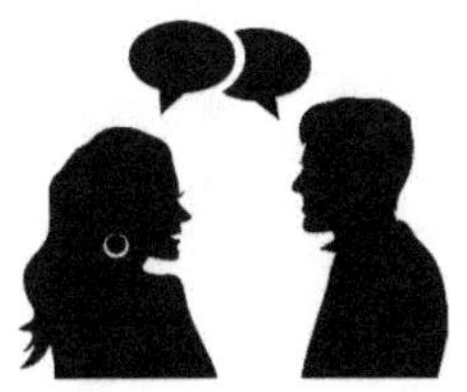

*Write how you feel about your date in the cloud image above.*

  

Congratulations On Completing The

# *Discovering Each Other Dating Activity Book*

## Book One

I hope you had fun together while sharing some insights about yourselves. Feel free to fill in the certificate on the following page to celebrate completing the activities in this book.

You may have found some interests you have in common and some beliefs and experiences that are very different. Don't let those differences discourage you if you both felt a connection to each other. Several scientific studies have shown that couples do not have to have identical interests to develop long term relationships.

Please visit the InwardVistas.com website if you'd like to learn more about the research behind some of the activities in this book.

Look for other books in the Drawing Closer Together™ series as you continue your journey toward a deeper understanding of yourself and toward complementing your life with loving relationships.

If you liked this book, I would appreciate your adding a review at the site where you obtained it so that others will know that it can be help support their self and relationship discoveries.

You can find out about new books published by Inward Vistas at InwardVistas.com.

  

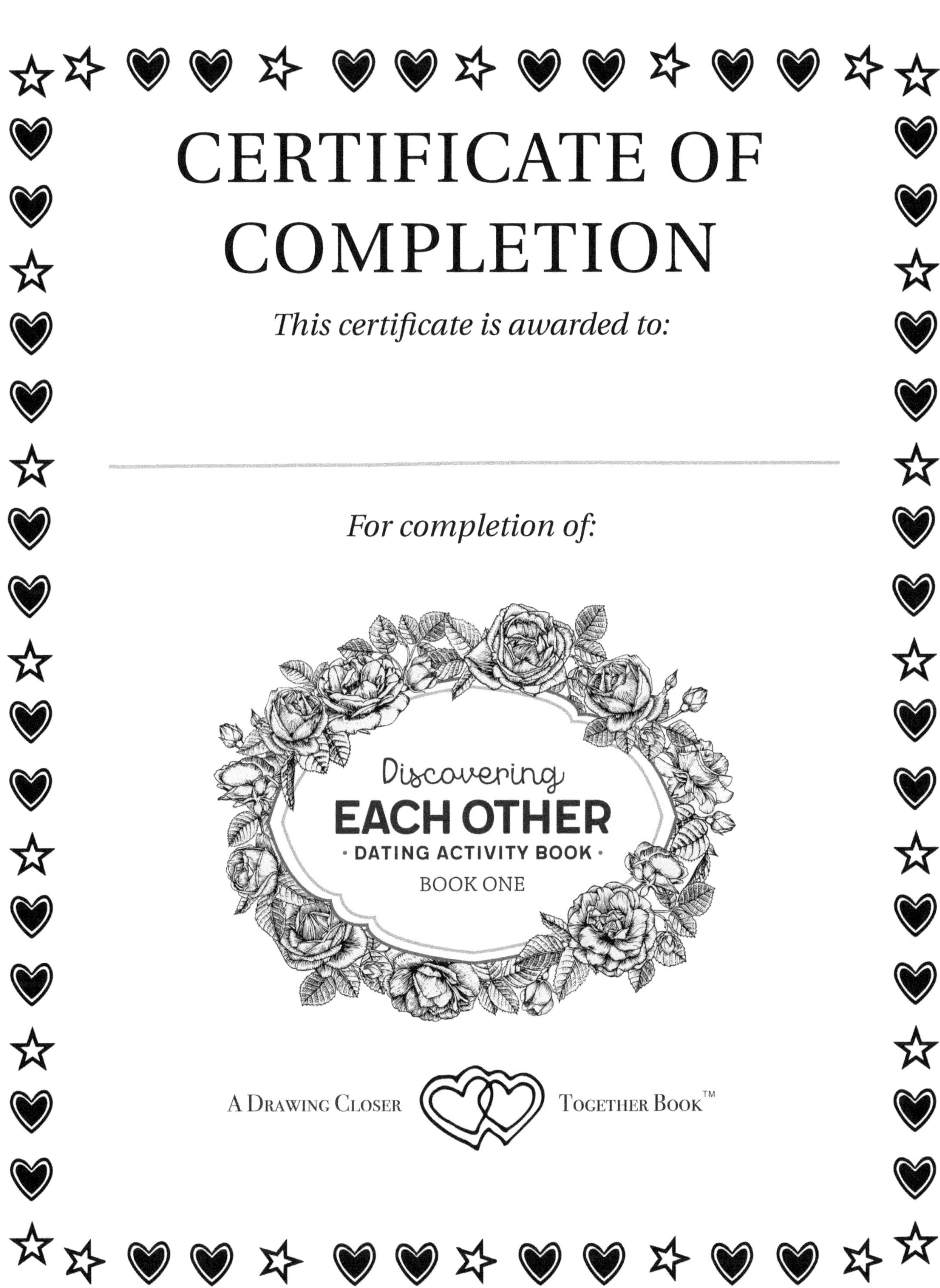
CERTIFICATE OF COMPLETION
This certificate is awarded to:
For completion of:
Discovering
EACH OTHER
· DATING ACTIVITY BOOK ·
BOOK ONE
A Drawing Closer Together Book™

# About the Author

ELLE DAHLMAN has a Master of Clinical Psychology degree from the University of California, Berkeley. Her studies included family relationships and the psychology of optimism. She loves using her background in psychology to inspire others.

She is working to increase the number of titles published in the Drawing Closer Together™ series, to help people on their journey of togetherness from dating to marriage to growing a family to living a full life.

She is a writer and speaker on topics related to education, career development, and marketing technology. She lives in the Midwest with her wonderful husband and two delightful boys.

Elle wants to hear from you. Please reach out to her to share your experiences with the books.


www.inwardvistas.com

Email: ElleDahlman@InwardVistas.com

Email list: Subscribe@InwardVistas.com


  

# Upcoming Titles In The Drawing Closer Together™ Series

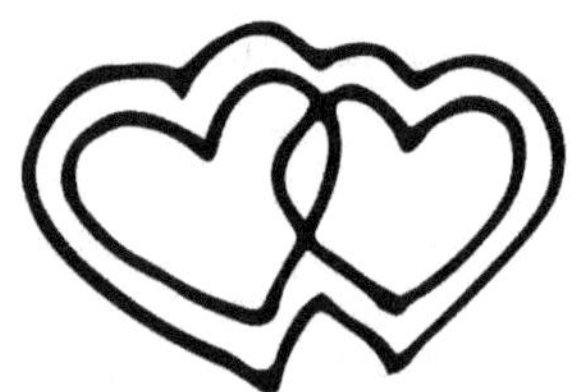

***Discovering Each Other Book Two***

***Getting Serious***

***Getting Ready to Date***

***Celebrating Our Love***

Join the InwardVistas email list at
Subscribe@InwardVistas.com
to stay in the loop about upcoming books.

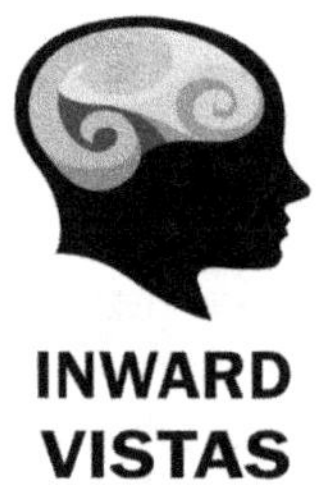

www.ingramcontent.com/pod-product-compliance
Lightning Source LLC
LaVergne TN
LVHW080337110826
845155LV00027B/256

* 9 7 8 1 9 4 5 0 3 7 0 6 1 *